IS
HEAVEN
FOR REAL?

IS HEAVEN FOR REAL?

CHRIS HOLLAND

Pacific Press®
Publishing Association

Nampa, Idaho | Oshawa, Ontario, Canada
www.pacificpress.com

Cover design by Gerald Lee Monks
Cover design resources from iStock-491844204 | Tijana87,
    iStock-539260759 | DNY59
Inside design by Aaron Troia

The author assumes full responsibility for the accuracy of all facts and
quotations as cited in this book.

Unless otherwise noted, Scripture quotations are taken from the New
King James Version®. Copyright © 1982 by Thomas Nelson. Used by
permission. All rights reserved.

Scripture quotations marked ESV are from The Holy Bible, English
Standard Version® (ESV®), copyright © 2001 by Crossway, a publishing ministry of Good News Publishers. Used by permission. All rights
reserved.

Scripture quotations marked KJV are from the King James Version.

Additional copies of this book are available for purchase by calling toll-
free 1-800-765-6955 or by visiting http://www.adventistbookcenter
.com.

Library of Congress Cataloging-in-Publication Data

Names: Holland, Chris (Director of It Is Written Canada), author.
Title: Is heaven for real? / Chris Holland.
Description: Nampa : Pacific Press Publishing Association, 2018.
Identifiers: LCCN 2018003770 | ISBN 9780816363933 (pbk. : alk.
    paper)
Subjects: LCSH: Death—Religious aspects—Christianity. | Future
    life—Christianity. | Heaven—Religious aspects—Christianity.
Classification: LCC BT825 .H765 2018 | DDC 236/.24—dc23
LC record available at https://lccn.loc.gov/2018003770

March 2018

Dedication

I dedicate this book to my wife, Debbie, who helped show me the way to Jesus, who is the Way, the Truth, and the Life.

Contents

Introduction

The subject of heaven has occupied the minds of some of the greatest minds throughout history. Plato taught his *soma sema*. This Greek phrase literally means the body is a tomb. Plato's call was to reach a freer reality and have the "soul" break forth from the bodily tomb. Is this the true nature of heaven? Pythagoras, the famed philosopher known for the Pythagorean theorem of mathematics, also taught this idea of a soul escaping from the tomb of the body. The prominent theologian Augustine embraced these same theories and introduced them to Christianity. Others have taught that heaven is just symbolic, while still others teach that it is an idealistic attainment of a new level of existence. So what should we believe? Is heaven symbolic? Or is it a real place? Where is it? How do we get there? When will we get to go? In this small book, I will attempt to answer these questions and, ultimately, whether heaven is for real.

CHAPTER 1

A Beautiful, Real Place

What would you say if I told you about a pink lake? How about mountains with red, orange, blue, and gold formations? Or a cave with crystals as long as eleven meters (thirty-six feet)? These may sound impossible, but they are all real places on this earth.

The pink-water lake is Lake Retba near Dakar, Senegal, close to the Cap Vert Peninsula, which is the westernmost point of the African continent. Its pink color is caused by a particular kind of algae growing in the lake.

The multicolored mountains? They can be found in Gansu, China. Throughout the region, you will find wonderful rainbow-colored mountains and rock formations.

Those huge crystals are found in the Cave of Crystals in Chihuahua, Mexico. The cave's temperature hovers around a blistering 50 degrees Celsius (122 degrees Fahrenheit). In pictures, cave explorers look small standing next to the huge white crystals, and the beauty of such crystals is amazing.

All of these seemingly unreal places *are* real. They actually exist, even though their descriptions seem to suggest the impossible!

Is Heaven for Real?

What about heaven—a place that is often discussed in religious circles? Is heaven real? People have a lot to say about it, and some claim to have been there. But what does the Bible say about heaven? Is it an actual place? Is it a faraway floating sphere with clouds and babies playing harps? Let us discover the truth about it.

The words *heaven* and *heavens* appear more than 720 times in the Bible. It is important to note that these words can have different meanings, however. "Heaven and earth" together can refer to the entire universe, while the words *heaven* and *heavens* can refer to the sky, the stars, and the planets. Those two words can also signify the home of the righteous. So in the Bible, the word *heaven* can mean a physical place we can see or the place we cannot see that God calls home, depending on the context. For our purpose here, we will concern ourselves with the latter meaning—the home of the righteous that we cannot see.

Sometimes heaven is described in the Bible without using the actual word. This is the case when Jesus speaks of heaven and the preparations He is making there for us. Notice what He says in John 14:1–4, which is a text you might know well: "Let not your heart be troubled; you believe in God, believe also in Me. In My Father's house are many mansions; if it were not so, I would have told you. I go to prepare a place for you. And if I go and prepare a place for you, I will come again and receive you to Myself; that where I am, there you may be also. And where I go you know, and the way you know." Here heaven is described as the place where God dwells. Jesus is preparing for His followers to go and settle there.

In our study, we will discover the wonderful home Jesus is preparing, keeping in mind what Isaiah says: "Since the beginning of the world men have not heard, nor perceived by the ear, neither hath the eye seen, O God, beside thee, what he hath prepared for him that waiteth for him" (Isaiah 64:4, KJV).

The Bible describes heaven in human terms so that we can understand, but those depictions fall short of how amazing it will be. Ephesians 3:20 says that God is "able to do exceedingly abundantly above all that we ask or think." So why even try to understand? Because heaven is an important place for us to know about, and we do not want to miss out on it.

God tells us how He will make our final home: "For behold, I create new heavens and a new earth; and the former shall not be remembered or come to mind" (Isaiah 65:17). He will make everything new. In Revelation, John describes it this way: "Now I saw a new heaven and a new earth, for the first heaven and the first earth had passed away" (Revelation 21:1).

God created this earth more than six thousand years ago, and He created it over the course of six days. It was perfect in every aspect. Then sin marred the earth, and now we are in the situation we find today—on a very imperfect planet. But a day is coming when God will destroy this earth to make a new earth on which we will live. On that day, there will be a lot of noise and physical and chemical reactions. "The day of the Lord will come as a thief in the night, in which the heavens will pass away with a great noise, and the elements will melt with fervent heat; both the earth and the works that are in it will be burned up" (2 Peter 3:10). Every aspect of this world will be destroyed and replaced: "The heavens will be dissolved, being on fire, and the elements will melt with fervent heat" (verse 12). "Nevertheless we, according to His promise, look for new heavens and a new earth in which righteousness dwells" (verse 13).

Heaven is God's home now. But where is it? The Bible does not give us an exact location. It is out in the universe somewhere. Psalm 14:2 says, "The LORD looks down from heaven upon the children of men, to see if there are any who understand, who seek God." And Psalm 33:13 says, "The LORD looks from heaven; He sees all the sons of men." God can see us from where He is, even though we cannot see Him. And describing Jesus' ascension from this earth, the book of Acts says, "Now when He had spoken these things, while they [the disciples] watched, He was taken up, and a cloud received Him out of their sight. And while they looked steadfastly toward heaven as He went up, behold, two men stood by them in white apparel, who also said, 'Men of Galilee, why do you stand gazing up into heaven? This same Jesus, who was taken up from you into heaven, will so come in like manner as you saw Him go into heaven'" (Acts 1:9–11). So heaven is a real place where God the Father lives, and Jesus is there too.

John tells us what he saw in vision when the city of

A Beautiful, Real Place

God will come to the remade earth: "Then I, John, saw the holy city, New Jerusalem, coming down out of heaven from God, prepared as a bride adorned for her husband" (Revelation 21:2). The city will come from heaven to earth. So where is heaven? It is out there somewhere. Heaven is a real place.

God made this earth so that He could be with His human friends. We rebelled and turned away from Him, and the earth was ruined. He will make it perfect again, with a guarantee, according to Nahum 1:9, that "affliction will not rise up a second time."

Heaven is a real place where there will not be any sin. No more drive-by shootings, no more car accidents, no more drunk drivers, and no more calls at midnight telling us about a family member who has died; nothing like that will happen anymore—forever.

The book of Revelation tells us what else will not be in heaven: pain and suffering. "God will wipe away every tear from their eyes; there shall be no more death, nor sorrow, nor crying. There shall be no more pain, for the former things have passed away" (Revelation 21:4). Heaven might seem too good to be true, but truly there will not be any more death—no more goodbyes, no more sudden losses, and no more heartache. If you have lost someone close to you, you'll be reunited. And because of that, there will be no more sorrow or grief. You will never have to mourn again.

Can you picture that perfect harmony? We will have no need to weep. No more tears of sadness; everything will be perfect in Jesus. Unquestionably, there will be no physical pain: no arthritis, and no aches and pains. Are you happy to know that? I know I am. I have had four knee surgeries, and I look forward to the day when there will be no aches and pains.

We are also talking about emotional pain. Maybe you have been abused, or you have gone through a traumatic time that left you emotionally damaged. Jesus reaches out His arms of love and tells you heaven is real. He says, "I am preparing a place for you right now! Cling to Me, stay close to Me, and I will take you there."

And God's people have heard the invitation. "Now they desire a better, that is, a heavenly country. Therefore God is not ashamed to be called their God, for He has prepared a city for them" (Hebrews 11:16). God has prepared heaven with you in mind.

Heaven has real gates for entry. Look at John's marvelous description in Revelation 21 of what the heavenly city looks like: An angel "showed me the great city, the holy Jerusalem, descending out of heaven from God, having the glory of God. Her light was like a most precious stone, like a jasper stone, clear as crystal. Also she had a great and high wall with twelve gates, and twelve angels at the gates, and names written on them, which are the names of the twelve tribes of the children of Israel: three gates on the east, three gates on the north, three gates on the south, and three gates on the west" (verses 10–13). These gates are not to keep anyone out but rather are a message for people to come from all corners of the earth and inhabit this place. Three gates to the north and to the south, to the west and to the east—twelve total—all cry out as an invitation to come into this beautiful place.

Revelation 21:14–17 also records the measurements of this magnificent city: "Now the wall of the city had twelve foundations, and on them were the names of the twelve apostles of the Lamb. And he who talked with me had a gold reed to measure the city, its gates, and its wall. The city is laid out as a square; its length is as great as its breadth. And he measured the city with the reed: twelve thousand furlongs. Its length, breadth, and height are equal. Then he measured its wall: one hundred and forty-four cubits, according to the measure of a man, that is, of an angel." Heaven has real foundations, which have the names of the apostles inscribed on them. And the city is a perfect square. Twelve thousand furlongs is just over 2,200 kilometers (1,367 miles), making the city a little more than 550 kilometers (342 miles) per side. That would be the equivalent of driving from downtown Toronto to Montreal—and that is just one side! It would be comparable to the distance between Calgary and Saskatoon or Calgary and Kamloops. And picture this: each side, 550 kilometers (342 miles) long, has a wall almost 64 meters (210 feet) thick. Heaven is a real, measurable place.

The building materials of the city are likewise impressive:

The construction of its wall was of jasper; and the city was pure gold, like clear glass. The foundations of the wall of the city were adorned with all kinds of precious stones: the first foundation was jasper, the second sapphire, the third chalcedony, the fourth emerald, the fifth sardonyx, the sixth sardius, the seventh chrysolite, the eighth beryl, the ninth topaz, the tenth chrysoprase, the eleventh jacinth, and the twelfth amethyst. The twelve gates were twelve pearls: each individual gate was of one pearl. And the street of the city was pure gold, like transparent glass (verses 18–21).

Picture that perfect beauty in your mind. Jesus has prepared all of this for you and me. Are you excited? This will be a city like you have never seen. No more pollution and no more terrible weather—instead, it will be absolute perfection.

In addition to the city of New Jerusalem on this earth made anew, we will also live in homes that we build in the countryside.

"They shall build houses and inhabit them;
They shall plant vineyards and eat their fruit.
They shall not build and another inhabit;
They shall not plant and another eat;
For as the days of a tree, so shall be the days of My people,
And My elect shall long enjoy the work of their hands" (Isaiah 65:21, 22).

A Beautiful, Real Place

We will build houses, plant gardens, and enjoy the fruits of our labor. No more will we build our dream homes only to move away and sell them. No more will we have beautiful gardens destroyed by weeds and pests. We will enjoy our lives in this very real place.

Our bodies also will be new. We will be able to work all day and not experience exhaustion and pain. Here is how Paul reports it: "For our citizenship is in heaven, from which we also eagerly wait for the Savior, the Lord Jesus Christ, who will transform our lowly body that it may be conformed to His glorious body, according to the working by which He is able even to subdue all things to Himself" (Philippians 3:20, 21).

So that we are sure this means our real physical bodies, think about what Jesus' body was like after He was resurrected from death. He appeared to His disciples and said,

> "Why are you troubled? And why do doubts arise in your hearts? Behold My hands and My feet, that it is I Myself. Handle Me and see, for a spirit does not have flesh and bones as you see I have."
>
> When He had said this, He showed them His hands and His feet (Luke 24:38–40).

In His remade body, Jesus was real flesh and bones. His lowly body was now glorious. It would never grow old. And it would not grow weary and stop working. Likewise, in that moment when we are re-created to live in heaven, our bodies will be perfect and imperishable.

In case you have not gotten the picture yet, notice that we will not be sitting around on clouds, strumming our harps. In heaven, real people will have real conversations. Jesus told us that "many will come from east and west, and sit down with Abraham, Isaac, and Jacob in the kingdom of heaven" (Matthew 8:11). Can you imagine what it will be like to have a conversation face-to-face with these heroes of the Bible? Think about who you would like to talk with first: Daniel, Jeremiah, Ruth, Matthew, David, or Joshua. Who will it be?

In addition, the perfect harmony of heaven will be seen in the animal kingdom. Isaiah shares a beautiful scene:

"The wolf also shall dwell with the lamb,
The leopard shall lie down with the young goat,
The calf and the young lion and the fatling together;
And a little child shall lead them.
The cow and the bear shall graze;
Their young ones shall lie down together;
And the lion shall eat straw like the ox.
The nursing child shall play by the cobra's hole,
And the weaned child shall put his hand in the viper's den.
They shall not hurt nor destroy in all My holy mountain,
For the earth shall be full of the knowledge of the LORD" (Isaiah 11:6–9).

All the animals will live in perfect harmony and peace. No animals will eat one another; instead, all of them will enjoy the peace of God.

Above all else, one thing in heaven that should attract us and bring us supreme joy is the opportunity to meet Jesus. He is the reason we will be there. He has made the provision for us to go, and He has prepared a place for us. Today He is calling you and me to prepare for entry into heaven—to come to Him, to give our lives to Him, to live for Him, and to be obedient to Him.

The Bible promises we will each receive a crown in heaven. Paul tells us, "There is laid up for me the crown of righteousness, which the Lord, the righteous Judge, will give to me on that Day, and not to me only but also to all who have loved His appearing" (2 Timothy 4:8). What a glorious day that will be!

Jesus has paid the price for us to enter heaven. He has invited you; it does not matter whether you are rich or poor, male or female, young or old, or successful or not. Jesus is calling you. He wants you to be prepared for heaven—a real place for real people. When we get there, we will receive a crown, but we will not even glory in that crown. Revelation 4 says that those in heaven cast their crowns at the feet of Jesus. Why? Because He paid the price for it all. Jesus calls you today. Will you answer?

CHAPTER 2

When Do We Get to Go?

There is no doubt that the Bible teaches that heaven is a real place. The question many people have is, When do we get to go there? Some say it happens the moment we die; others say there is a waiting time in purgatory; and yet others assert that it happens when Jesus comes back to this earth. So when exactly do we get to go to heaven?

To find our answer, let us go on a journey back to ancient Egypt. In ancient Egypt's culture and religion, the afterlife was very important. Some of the greatest monuments and treasures found in Egypt were created because of the people's understanding of the afterlife. This viewpoint is apparent when visiting some of the ancient Egyptians' tombs. In them, we find coffins nested, one inside another; and the innermost coffin contains the embalmed body of the deceased. The embalming process involved removing all of the body's fluids, and often all of the organs except the heart, and then wrapping the body. Included in that wrapping would be a copy of the Book of the Dead.

The Book of the Dead was not a bound book as we think of books today but rather a papyrus scroll. The Book of the Dead was, in the Egyptian custom, a set of inscriptions that were meant to guard and protect the spirit of the dead person. As Egyptologists worked to decipher the book, they found a description of a ceremony called the weighing of the heart. This was an act performed by the gods: they weighed the heart to determine a person's destiny; the good deeds were measured against the bad deeds in a person's life.

Aren't you glad that Jesus does not work that way? He does not list our works and find that we have done 600 good deeds but then finds 601 bad deeds and banishes us forever. Jesus stands for us, and as long as we have given our lives to Him, He will save us. His grace is freely received and can save us from eternal death.

The Egyptians did not believe death was the end of existence. During the Egyptian process of preparing a body for embalming, the deceased's mouth would be opened so he or she would again be able to eat, drink, breathe, and speak. In the fifth century B.C., the historian Herodotus wrote, "The Egyptians were the first who maintained the following doctrine . . . that the human soul is immortal, and at the death of the body enters into some other living thing then coming to birth; and after passing through all creatures of land, sea, and air, it enters once more into a human body at birth, a cycle which it completes in three thousand years. There are Greeks who have used this doctrine, some earlier and some later, as if it were their own."[1]

Here we begin to see why the understandings of what happens at death and when we go to heaven are such important topics. We see the emergence of two lines of thinking: the pagan doctrine of an immortal soul conceived by the Egyptians and adopted by some Greeks, which would become known as dualism and, in contrast, what the Bible teaches about immortality and the afterlife. The two streams of thought are human thoughts and ideas versus God's truth. The question is, Which will we believe and follow?

So what happens when we die? And when do we go to heaven? The only reliable answers on these topics are found in God's Word.

The only way to understand what happens to a person when he or she dies is to know how life begins. Genesis 2:7 says, "The Lord God formed man of the dust of the ground, and breathed into his nostrils the breath of life; and man became a living being." The King James Version says that man "became a living soul." Notice the simple formula used here: God took the dust of the ground to make the man, then He breathed into his nostrils the breath of life, and the man became a living soul. Notice that the man does not *have* a soul but rather he *is* a soul.

The equation is not that complicated—the elements of the earth plus the breath of God equal a living being. The soul is not a separate conscious entity but rather is the whole being. So the word *soul*, we could say, simply means a person.

Some say that the soul is immortal. But from a biblical point of view, that is not the case. Ezekiel 18:4 is quite clear: "The soul who sins shall die." So the soul is not an immortal entity, because a soul can die. Some of the modern versions of the Bible translate that verse to say that the *person* who sins shall die.

In the Bible, the word *soul* is used in one of two ways. If the Bible is talking about *soul* as the product of body and spirit together—God formed man out of the dust of the ground, and God breathed into his nostrils the breath of life—then it means a living soul, a living person, a living being. On the other hand, where the Bible talks about the soul as something a person has, it refers to life, or the very essence and core of who a person is.

But the soul is not immortal. The Bible says plainly that not one of us is inherently immortal. First Timothy 6:15, 16 states clearly, "The King of kings and Lord of lords, who alone has immortality." This is a very important point: God alone has immortality, and no one else has it. The Bible uses the word *soul* more than fifteen hundred times, and not once is it used in the context of an immortal soul. Notice how Jesus Himself uses the word *soul* in Matthew 16:24–26. He said to His disciples, "If anyone desires to come after Me, let him deny himself, and take up his cross, and follow Me. For whoever desires to save his life will lose it, but whoever loses his life for My sake will find it. For what profit is it to a man if he gains the whole world, and loses his own soul? Or what will a man give in exchange for his soul?" Notice how Jesus uses the words *life* and *soul* interchangeably. The *soul* is never immortal in the Bible. It is a description of the very life of an individual and not some separate immortal entity. Job 4:17 says, "Can a mortal be more righteous than God? Can a man be more pure than his Maker?" Here human beings are called "mortal" and therefore cannot be immortal. And Paul tells us that "eternal life [comes] to those who by patient continuance in doing good seek for glory, honor, and immortality" (Romans 2:7). Immortality is what we receive as our reward at the moment of Jesus' return.

Please take note that the scripture is clear that we *seek* immortality. We would not need to seek it if we already possessed it. We are not naturally immortal. This is why Paul tells us that it will happen someday: "Behold, I tell you a mystery: We shall not all sleep, but we shall all be changed—in a moment, in the twinkling of an eye, at the last trumpet. For the trumpet will sound, and the dead will be raised incorruptible, and we shall be changed. For this corruptible must put on incorruption, and this mortal must put on immortality. So when this corruptible has put on incorruption, and this mortal has put on immortality, then shall be brought to pass the saying that is written: 'Death is swallowed up in victory'" (1 Corinthians 15:51–54). These are God's words about immortality. When does He say that it will happen? At the last trumpet. When is that trumpet blown? First Thessalonians 4:16, 17 describes when this event will take place: at the second coming of Jesus. The Bible is clear that God the Father, the Son, and the Holy Spirit alone are in possession of eternal life, and immortality is not granted to any human being until the Second Coming.

Over the centuries, Greek and pagan dualism entered the church and brought in the false teaching that the body and soul are separate entities and that the soul exists eternally. In contrast, the Bible clearly delineates that a person is a soul or a living being and very much mortal.

The false idea of the immortal soul in Christianity was condemned by ancient historians. The early Christian writer Justin Martyr, who lived only one generation after the disciples of Jesus, said these words: "If you have fallen in with some who are called Christians, but who do not admit this [truth of the resurrection] and venture to blaspheme the God of Abraham, and the God of Isaac, and the God of Jacob; who say there is no resurrection of the dead, and that their souls when they die, are taken to heaven; do not imagine that they are Christians."[2] These are strong words about an error that entered the church in the early days. Justin Martyr demonstrated the biblical understanding that a soul is a living person and that a person is mortal and shall die.

So if the Christian church did not teach that a person would go to heaven immediately after death, what does the Bible teach about death? We find that the Bible teaches that death is merely creation in reverse. It is simply an unconscious sleep—a period of waiting for the return of Jesus. Ecclesiastes 12:7 describes it: "Then the dust will return to the earth as it was, and the spirit will return to God who gave it." Death is the cessation of life and entering into an unconscious sleep, awaiting the return of Jesus.

What does the Bible mean by the "spirit" that returns to God? In ancient Hebrew, the word for "spirit" and the word for "breath" are the same. It is the Hebrew word *ruach.* The "spirit" or "breath" is simply a reference to God's life-giving power. When a person dies, that power returns to Him, and the being that was alive ceases to exist until Jesus comes again. Notice in Job 27:3 that the words *spirit* and *breath* are used interchangeably in the King James Version, as well as in other versions: "All the while my breath is in me, and the spirit of God is in my nostrils." This interchangeable use demonstrates that the spirit or breath is the life-giving power of God. We cannot live without it. James 2:26 says, "For as the body without the spirit is dead, so faith without works is dead also." There is no in-between state—no spirit-life. Once we die, we are asleep and wait for the wake-up call of Jesus.

Let us compare the process to building a box. To build a box, you need some boards and screws. The formula for building a box is easy: boards + screws = box. Take away the screws and all you have is boards; take away the boards and all you have is screws. Put them together in the right way and you have a box. But without both components put together, the box simply ceases to exist. Human existence works the same way. When we die, the components are not together anymore, and we rest. We are not living beings anymore. We no longer have life. The life goes back to God. For the believer, it is like resting in the arms of Jesus, resting secure in His love. There is no conscious thought until the day that Jesus will come back. In that moment, in the twinkling of an eye, Jesus will bring life back to us, and we will be resurrected from the dead.

Here is how the Bible describes it. Psalm 146:4 says,

When Do We Get to Go?

"His spirit departs, he returns to his earth; in that very day his plans perish." When a person dies, one's plans and thoughts cease. There is no more conscious existence. Ecclesiastes 9:5, 6 offers further insight:

> For the living know that they will die;
> But the dead know nothing,
> And they have no more reward,
> For the memory of them is forgotten.
> Also their love, their hatred, and their envy have now
>   perished;
> Nevermore will they have a share
> In anything done under the sun.

The dead know *nothing*. Their thoughts stop, and their emotions stop. Why? Because death is a sleep, where we wait unconsciously for Jesus. Thank God that your dead loved ones do not have to witness you facing the sorrows of this life. A loved one who died of cancer no longer suffers; instead, he or she is sleeping, resting until the glorious day of the resurrection. We can be thankful that death is not the end. You will again see that husband who died in Jesus. You will again see that wife who died in Jesus. On that glorious day, you will again see that mother, father, son, or daughter who died in Jesus.

When Jesus Christ comes again, there will be a powerful resurrection, and all who have believed and followed Jesus will be raised from the dead with immortal bodies. Any of us who are still alive on that day will receive our immortal bodies also and will be caught up in the air with them to meet Christ. Until then, death is but a sleep. The psalmist wrote, "Consider and hear me, O LORD my God; enlighten my eyes, lest I sleep the sleep of death" (Psalm 13:3). "The dead do not praise the LORD, nor any who go down into silence" (Psalm 115:17). "For in death there is no remembrance of You; in the grave who will give You thanks?" (Psalm 6:5). Death is a peaceful sleep awaiting Jesus.

This idea of death may be new to you, and it may be unsettling. I encourage you to study your Bible on this topic and draw near to Jesus. Ask the Holy Spirit for guidance. I know there are other questions: What about the thief on the cross? What about Lazarus? What about those who say they have had near-death experiences? We will answer all those questions in this book.

Let us be thankful to Jesus that in His mercy and grace, He came to save us. Let us be thankful that death is like a sleep and is not forever. It is not, like the atheist says, simply a time of nothingness, and that the dead will never exist again. God's truth is that death is a temporary pause that only Jesus can release. He is our wonderful and merciful Savior.

1. Herodotus, *The Histories* 2.123.2, 2.123.3.
2. Justin Martyr, *Dialogue With Trypho* 80, in *The Ante-Nicene Fathers*, ed. Alexander Roberts and James Donaldson, vol. 1 (New York: Charles Scribner's Sons, 1905), 239.

CHAPTER 3

What Jesus Said About
Death and Resurrection

Steven Sykes was born in England in 1914. He is best known for his work as an artist, especially in the Gethsemane Chapel in Coventry Cathedral, also referred to as St. Michael's Cathedral, in England. During World War II, Sykes joined the British army and worked in the camouflage unit. At a most critical juncture in the war, Sykes was commissioned to help camouflage the building of a railway from the Mediterranean Sea to Misheifa in Egypt. How would he actually hide a railway? Sykes devised an ingenious plan. Instead of camouflaging the railway itself, Sykes decided to build a fake railhead. His commanding officer approved the idea. Sykes and his team took leftover wood, palm fronds, and gas cans to form this false railway and railhead. The rails, buildings, even wooden tanks were included in his grand scheme. On November 22, 1941, the test came when enemy bombers flew overhead. They believed what they were seeing and bombed the fake railhead and its accessories. Sykes's team was hidden nearby and set off flares to make the scene look like burning wreckage, furthering the deception. Meanwhile, the real railway and railhead were built and used successfully. The entire scheme was based on deception.

The art of deceiving is based on subtle lies. Could it be that over the centuries Christianity has been deceived into believing one of the original subtle lies of the devil? "The serpent [the devil] said to the woman [Eve], 'You will not surely die. For God knows that in the day you eat of it your eyes will be opened, and you will be like God, knowing good and evil'" (Genesis 3:4, 5). This was a false promise that the woman would become like God. The devil made these promises also: (1) that even in disobedience she would not die and (2) that her eyes would be opened and, ultimately, she would be like God, knowing good and evil.

Here we see that one of the devil's subtle lies was the promise of immortality. But the Bible is clear in 1 Timothy 6:16 when it describes God: He "alone has immortality." God alone inherently possesses eternal life. Human beings must put on eternal life, as promised in 1 Corinthians 15:54: "So when this corruptible has put on incorruption, and this mortal has put on immortality, then shall be brought to pass the saying that is written: 'Death is swallowed up in victory.'" Even when we receive the gift of immortality from the Lord, we will still be forever dependent upon Him for life.

We have been asking the question, Is heaven for real? In a thorough study of the Scriptures, we discover two very important things: First, the Bible says that a human being does not have a soul; he or she *is* a soul. Second, we see again and again that the Bible refers to death as a sleep that lasts until Christ's second coming. The Bible mentions death as a sleep more than fifty times. A typical example is Psalm 13:3, "Consider and hear me, O Lord my God; enlighten my eyes, lest I sleep the sleep of death." David understood that death was a sleep. Peter, in his famous sermon at Pentecost, spoke of King David this way: "Men and brethren, let me speak freely to you of the patriarch David, that he is both dead and buried, and his tomb is with us to this day" (Acts 2:29). A few verses later he says, "For David did not ascend into the heavens" (verse 34). In the Old Testament, David taught and believed that death was a sleep; and in the New Testament, Peter believed and taught that death was a sleep.

What did Jesus teach about death? It is no surprise that He taught that death is a sleep. You may remember Jesus' friend Lazarus, who became sick and died. Lazarus had been dead for four days when Jesus and His disciples arrived at the man's home. Before they set out on the journey, Jesus had said,

> "Our friend Lazarus sleeps, but I go that I may wake him up."
> Then His disciples said, "Lord, if he sleeps he will get well." However, Jesus spoke of his death, but they thought that He was speaking about taking rest in sleep.

Then Jesus said to them plainly, "Lazarus is dead" (John 11:11–14).

The disciples thought that if Jesus was going to wake Lazarus out of sleep, Lazarus must be doing pretty well, perhaps even getting better. But notice how Jesus uses these words interchangeably. First, He said, "Lazarus sleeps." Then He said, "Lazarus is dead." So in Jesus' mind, death was a sleep.

The idea that the soul lives on outside of the body is derived from Greek dualism, which was inherited from Egyptian mystical religions. I do not know about you, but I would rather learn about death from Jesus and His Word than from Egyptian, Babylonian, or Greek philosophy.

When Jesus drew near Bethany, He sent word and met with Martha and then Mary, Lazarus's sisters. Naturally, they were mourning the loss of their brother.

Martha, in her distress, said to Jesus, "Lord, if You had been here, my brother would not have died. But even now I know that whatever You ask of God, God will give You" (verses 21, 22). Jesus reassured Martha with these words: "Your brother will rise again" (verse 23). Now Martha knew the Scriptures and answered Him, "I know that he will rise again in the resurrection at the last day" (verse 24). She did not speak of Lazarus as being in heaven, nor did she speak of any joyful bliss he was experiencing. Instead, she looked forward to the last day of earth's history, when Jesus would raise Lazarus from the dead.

Jesus responded with these powerful words: "I am the

resurrection and the life. He who believes in Me, though he may die, he shall live. And whoever lives and believes in Me shall never die. Do you believe this?" (verses 25, 26). He meant that death cannot snatch away our assurance of eternal life. Martha knew her brother would rise again, but more specifically, she knew that he was going to rise in the resurrection on the last day. She did not say, "Oh, Jesus, my brother is up in heaven," or "My brother is looking down at me now." She knew that Lazarus was sleeping until the day that Jesus Christ would come and raise him from the dead. That is what the Bible teaches.

Jesus holds the keys to the tomb. He is the only one who can hit the Resume button from the temporary pause of death. He also knew that He would go into the grave and that He would come out. Death cannot hold Him. And He assured Martha that if the tomb could not hold Him, it would not be able to hold her brother either.

Then Jesus did something amazing. As a testimony that He could raise the dead and that millions will be raised when He comes again, as a testimony that the grave cannot hold those people who have dedicated their lives to Him, He purposefully went to Lazarus's tomb.

Then Jesus, again groaning in Himself, came to the tomb. It was a cave, and a stone lay against it. Jesus said, "Take away the stone."

Martha, the sister of him who was dead, said to Him, "Lord, by this time there is a stench, for he has been dead four days" (verses 38, 39).

Is Heaven for Real?

Martha was concerned that Lazarus was already decomposing and there would be a smell.

> Jesus said to her, "Did I not say to you that if you would believe you would see the glory of God?" Then they took away the stone from the place where the dead man was lying. And Jesus lifted up His eyes and said, "Father, I thank You that You have heard Me. And I know that You always hear Me, but because of the people who are standing by I said this, that they may believe that You sent Me." Now when He had said these things, He cried with a loud voice, "Lazarus, come forth!" And he who had died came out bound hand and foot with graveclothes, and his face was wrapped with a cloth. Jesus said to them, "Loose him, and let him go" (verses 40–44).

As Lazarus came out of the tomb, the people gathered around were stunned.

Let me be very clear: if Jesus raised Lazarus, He can raise your husband, your wife, your son or daughter, your brother or sister, your aunt or uncle—Jesus will raise from the dead those who have followed Him. Death is not the end.

Notice also from this story that if, as a lot of people believe, we go straight to heaven or hell at death, one would think that Lazarus would have had a lot more to say than he did. Think about it. Lazarus would have been up in heaven for four days. Don't you think that when Jesus said, "Come forth!" Lazarus would have said, "Lord, I am not coming back. I want to stay up here in the glory land and eat the fruit of the tree of life. I want to stay with the angels. I just cannot return"? If anybody could have written a bestseller, it would have been Lazarus and his tale of the afterlife. But there is no mention of what heaven was like or of a near-death experience. Why did he not share any stories like that? Because he was sleeping and did not know anything. "For the living know that they will die; but the dead know nothing" (Ecclesiastes 9:5).

The resurrection of Lazarus is proof that Jesus Christ will someday resurrect our believing loved ones too. The grave could not hold Lazarus, and the grave cannot hold your loved ones. You need not fear death, because the grave cannot hold you.

The book of Job says that a dead man's "sons come to honor, and he does not know it; they are brought low, and he does not perceive it" (Job 14:21). Lazarus did not know the pain of his sisters and his friends while he was sleeping in death. When we die, the later events on earth are unknown to us.

Now some will say, "I like to think of Mama up there, looking down at me," or "I like to think of Daddy looking down at me." While I understand the appeal of this thought, let us think this through further. Imagine a young boy playing baseball with his friends. Someone hits the ball over the fence, and it goes out into the road. The boy runs after it, and then *screech!* The driver of a car tries to stop, but the boy is knocked down. He is now a paraplegic and lies in pain for the rest of his life. If it were true that his mother goes to heaven when she dies, she would be looking down on her son lying in pain for the rest of his life after she is gone. Would she be happy up in heaven if she did that? Or imagine a soldier whose father has died before he goes to war. The young soldier gets caught behind enemy lines, and they gouge out his eyes. They torture him mercilessly. If his father were in heaven already, he would be watching what happens to his son. Is that what the Bible teaches?

God's way is much better. Those who have died are protected from all of that pain. We die, and there is no more suffering or pain. We rest. And like the experience of sleep, in death we have no sense of the passage of time. The next thing we will know is Jesus Christ coming for us on the day of the resurrection.

King David described when he would receive his new body in Psalm 17:15, "I shall be satisfied when I awake in Your likeness." And Paul describes when that day will be: "I have fought the good fight, I have finished the race, I have kept the faith. Finally, there is laid up for me the crown of righteousness, which the Lord, the righteous Judge, will give to me on that Day, and not to me only but also to all who have loved His appearing" (2 Timothy 4:7, 8). Jesus promised, "Behold, I am coming quickly, and My reward is with Me, to give to every one according to his work" (Revelation 22:12). That reward is not at death but when He comes again.

What Jesus Said About Death and Resurrection

I am thankful that in death we do not experience the sorrows of life. I am thankful that my friends who died of cancer no longer suffer but are sleeping until the glorious day of the resurrection. I am thankful that death is not the end. You can see your loved ones when Christ comes back again. On that glorious morning, those who have been believers and followers of Jesus will be raised from the dead with immortal bodies. We who are alive will receive our immortal bodies and will be caught up together with them to meet Christ in the air.

Wouldn't it be a tragedy if your mother or father were looking for you on that day and you were not there? Wouldn't it be a tragedy if your brother or sister or son or daughter were looking for you and you were not there— lost for all eternity? The greatest tragedy would be if Jesus were looking for you and you were not there. He wants to save you in His kingdom forever. He will feel an emptiness in His heart if you are not in heaven with Him.

One day soon Christ will come. The sky will be illuminated with the glory of God. The earth will shake, and the graves will open. Death will be defeated forever. God will give us immortal bodies, and we'll ascend through the sky. And Jesus is looking for you. The gleams of the golden morning will come. Do not miss it.

Do you want to be there? Why not pray now and say, "Jesus, I want to be there. If I die before You come, Lord, I want to fall asleep knowing that the grave will be opened. I want the next voice I hear to be Jesus' voice. I want the next thing I see to be Jesus' face. Lord, I want to be reunited with my family and friends. I want to see Jesus."

Why not think about that scene and give your heart to Jesus right now?

CHAPTER 4

The Importance of a Comma

Len and Nicole Clamp wanted to experience the joy of raising a child and were given the opportunity through foster parenting. Eventually, Grayson joined their family when he was only seven weeks old. They noticed quickly that something was different about Grayson—he was completely deaf. The Clamps had Grayson for almost a year, and then they were given the opportunity to adopt him. Knowing he had an impairment, they decided that they could be the best parents for Grayson and went ahead with the adoption. As the boy grew, they learned different ways to communicate with him.

Grayson's deafness was caused by the absence of the nerves that connect the ear to the hearing center of the brain. Because of this, cochlear implants would not help him. But doctors working with the Clamps proposed a solution—an auditory brain stem implant. If Grayson was approved for the surgery, he would be the first child to receive such an implant in the United States.

The doctors at the University of North Carolina Medical Center carefully mapped out the surgery, which they then performed in April 2013. On May 21, they activated

Grayson's device, and he heard his father's voice for the very first time. In what has become a very popular online video, you can see the look of utter surprise on the boy's face.

Often when we learn new ideas, we are greatly surprised. Sometimes these are welcome surprises, and sometimes they are overwhelming. As we have answered whether heaven is for real, our study has led us to what the Bible says about what happens when you die. The conclusions of our study may have caused you great surprise. It may be a little shocking to realize that the Bible says when someone dies, he or she is asleep, awaiting the Lord's return. When I began studying the Bible and learned this for the very first time, I, too, was shocked—so shocked that it made me angry. How could I have been wrong for so long? But then I learned the origins of the idea of the soul going immediately to heaven or to hell. The concept that the body and soul exist apart from each other comes from Greek dualism, which was derived from an ancient Egyptian belief. But we are concerned only with what the Bible teaches.

To help us with the shock, we are going to study some misunderstood texts in the Bible. For example, I have people say to me, "Wait a second, what about the thief on the cross? Didn't Jesus say to the thief, 'Today you'll be with Me in Paradise'?"

You may find it amazing, but there are more than fifteen hundred passages in the Bible about the soul, and not one of them speaks of the immortal soul. Not one! They are all in harmony with the words of Solomon: "The living know that they will die; but the dead know nothing" (Ecclesiastes 9:5). Unfortunately, a number of people want to throw out hundreds of clear texts in the Bible about death, about the second coming of Christ, and about the resurrection so that they can accept ancient Greek and Egyptian ideas about the immortality of the soul.

A very important principle of Bible study is that we start with passages that are clear and then move on to passages that are more challenging to understand. We cannot base our beliefs on one or a few texts; rather, we must see all of the biblical evidence put together.

So what about that thief on the cross? The closing chapters of the Gospels of Matthew and Luke tell of the final moments in Jesus' life here on earth. Jesus was crucified between two thieves, and these two were not the finest of fellows. Matthew 27:38–44 says,

Then two robbers were crucified with Him, one on the right and another on the left.

And those who passed by blasphemed Him, wagging their heads and saying, "You who destroy the temple and build it in three days, save Yourself! If You are the Son of God, come down from the cross."

Likewise the chief priests also, mocking with the scribes and elders, said, "He saved others; Himself He cannot save. If He is the King of Israel, let Him now come down from the cross, and we will believe Him. He trusted in God; let Him deliver Him now if He will have Him; for He said, 'I am the Son of God.'"

Even the robbers who were crucified with Him reviled Him with the same thing.

Crucified on either side of Christ, both robbers reviled and insulted Jesus. But while those criminals were hanging next to Jesus, something began to happen. One of the thieves saw a completely innocent Man dying on the cross and yet that Man did not retaliate or complain. Jesus had even asked God to forgive the ones who persecuted Him. Luke tells the rest of the story:

Then one of the criminals who were hanged blasphemed Him, saying, "If You are the Christ, save Yourself and us."

But the other, answering, rebuked him, saying, "Do you not even fear God, seeing you are under the same condemnation? And we indeed justly, for we receive the due reward of our deeds; but this Man has done nothing wrong." Then he said to Jesus, "Lord, remember me when You come into Your kingdom" (Luke 23:39–42).

That thief began to experience the transformation of his heart. He looked at Jesus and saw Him as the Messiah of the world. He cried out, "Remember me when You come into Your kingdom."

How then does Jesus respond? "Jesus said to him,

The Importance of a Comma

'Assuredly, I say to you, today you will be with Me in Paradise'" (verse 43). And it is here that we have a misunderstood text.

What is this text really saying? Does Jesus tell the thief, "I say to you today, on this day that I have got the crown of thorns on My head and nails through My hands, this day that I am dying on the cross, when it does not look as though I can save anybody, on this very day, you will be with Me in Paradise"? Or is it possible that there is a different meaning to the text?

It all depends on where you put that comma. If you put it before the word *today*, the text seems to say that the thief would be in Paradise that very day. But if you put the comma after *today*, look at the difference of the meaning: "Assuredly, I say to you today, you will be with Me in Paradise." In other words, "This day I am hanging on the cross, this day with nails through My hands, I am making this statement to you today, that you will be with Me in Paradise." That is, you will be there in the future.

Somebody may ask, "When were the commas added?"

There were no commas in the original Greek text when it was written in the first century. The commas were put in thirteen hundred years later, during the Middle Ages.

Somebody else may ask, "How do you know where to put in the comma?" The rule of thumb is that we should place the comma where the thought will harmonize with the rest of the Bible.

The Bible cannot be broken. If the commas were not in the original text but were placed there thirteen hundred years later, and if indeed the Bible is very clear that death is a sleep until Jesus returns, then we must place the comma where it harmonizes with the rest of the Bible. We do not throw out the clear teaching of the Bible on the subject of death as a sleep and accept an Egyptian idea on the immortality of the soul based on one comma that was put in thirteen hundred years after the New Testament was written.

There is another reason why the comma has to be placed after the word *today* and not before. How could Christ promise the thief that he would be with Him in Paradise that day if Jesus Himself did not go to Paradise that day? This may come as a shock—Jesus did not go there after He died!

The Bible tells us that Jesus died on Preparation Day, Friday, which most of us know as Good Friday. The next day was the Sabbath, and Jesus rested in death in the tomb on the Sabbath. On the next day, Sunday, the first day of the week, called Easter Sunday by many, Jesus rose from the dead. Mary Magdalene went to the tomb to embalm Jesus' body; but she did not know He had risen from the dead. There, through her teary eyes, she saw the empty tomb. Then she saw someone she thought was the gardener. But it was Jesus.

> She, supposing Him to be the gardener, said to Him, "Sir, if You have carried Him away, tell me where You have laid Him, and I will take Him away."
> Jesus said to her, "Mary!"

The Importance of a Comma

She turned and said to Him, "Rabboni!" (which is to say, Teacher).

Jesus said to her, "Do not cling to Me, for I have not yet ascended to My Father; but go to My brethren and say to them, 'I am ascending to My Father and your Father, and to My God and your God'" (John 20:15–17).

Jesus said He had not yet ascended to His Father on Sunday. If He had not ascended at any time before Sunday, He would not have said to the thief on Friday that they would be together in Paradise that day. The comma makes the difference. I am thankful that Jesus' Word makes it plain. He was saying to the thief, "You do not need to fear death because you can have eternal life through My death on the cross."

Wherever you are today, you need not fear death. Because of Jesus' death on the cross, your sins can be forgiven.

"O Death, where is your sting?
O Hades, where is your victory?"

. . . But thanks be to God, who gives us the victory through our Lord Jesus Christ (1 Corinthians 15:55–57).

The tomb of Christ is empty, and our tombs can be opened up and emptied when Jesus Christ returns. The same Christ who ascended will descend. This is the lesson of the thief on the cross: we will rest in the grave with the assurance that Jesus Christ will come again to wake us up and take us home.

In another part of the Bible, it seems as though the dead prophet Samuel comes back to visit King Saul as a disembodied spirit. But again, we have seen the evidence that death is like a sleep. Let us see what the Bible actually says.

Saul said to his servants, "Find me a woman who is a medium, that I may go to her and inquire of her."

And his servants said to him, "In fact, there is a woman who is a medium at En Dor."

So Saul disguised himself and put on other clothes, and he went, and two men with him; and they came to the woman by night. And he said, "Please conduct a séance for me, and bring up for me the one I shall name to you."

Then the woman said to him, "Look, you know what Saul has done, how he has cut off the mediums and the spiritists from the land. Why then do you lay a snare for my life, to cause me to die?"

And Saul swore to her by the LORD, saying, "As the LORD lives, no punishment shall come upon you for this thing."

Then the woman said, "Whom shall I bring up for you?"

And he said, "Bring up Samuel for me."

When the woman saw Samuel, she cried out with a loud voice. And the woman spoke to Saul, saying,

The Importance of a Comma

"Why have you deceived me? For you are Saul!"

And the king said to her, "Do not be afraid. What did you see?"

And the woman said to Saul, "I saw a spirit ascending out of the earth."

So he said to her, "What is his form?"

And she said, "An old man is coming up, and he is covered with a mantle." And Saul perceived that it was Samuel, and he stooped with his face to the ground and bowed down.

Now Samuel said to Saul, "Why have you disturbed me by bringing me up?" (1 Samuel 28:7–15).

Note some important points here. First, Saul is acting in direct disobedience to God. In Deuteronomy 18:10–14, God forbids consulting with a medium:

"There shall not be found among you anyone who makes his son or his daughter pass through the fire, or one who practices witchcraft, or a soothsayer, or one who interprets omens, or a sorcerer, or one who conjures spells, or a medium, or a spiritist, or one who calls up the dead. For all who do these things are an abomination to the LORD, and because of these abominations the LORD your God drives them out from before you. You shall be blameless before the LORD your God. For these nations which you will dispossess listened to soothsayers and diviners; but as for you, the LORD your God has not appointed such for you."

God calls the art of witchcraft or attempting to call up the dead an abomination because it is in direct contradiction to His Word.

Second, the Bible says Saul perceived that it was Samuel, but could it have really been Samuel? Of course not. Remember Ecclesiastes 9:5,

> For the living know that they will die;
> But the dead know nothing,
> And they have no more reward,
> For the memory of them is forgotten.

The witch was using mystical practices that deceived Saul. This was not Samuel but a demonic being impersonating Samuel. "And no wonder! For Satan himself transforms himself into an angel of light" (2 Corinthians 11:14). Samuel was resting in his grave and could not be awakened by anyone other than Jesus.

Some say that Paul advocates for people going straight to heaven in 2 Corinthians 5:6–8. He writes, "We are always confident, knowing that while we are at home in the body we are absent from the Lord. For we walk by faith, not by sight. We are confident, yes, well pleased rather to be absent from the body and to be present with the Lord." But is Paul advocating for the soul's existence apart from the body? No, he is stating what the Bible clearly teaches: while in these mortal bodies, we are absent from the Lord. When will we be present with the Lord? Paul explains, "Behold, I tell you a mystery: We shall not all sleep, but we shall all be changed—in a moment, in the twinkling of an eye, at the last trumpet. For the trumpet will sound, and the dead will be raised incorruptible, and we shall be changed" (1 Corinthians 15:51, 52). Only at the last trumpet are we raised incorruptible and present with the Lord. Again Paul is clear in 2 Timothy 4:8: "Finally, there is laid up for me the crown of righteousness, which the Lord, the righteous Judge, will give to me on that Day, and not to me only but also to all who have loved His appearing." We are present with God and receive that crown of righteousness after the second coming of Jesus. Until that time, we rest in the grave waiting for Jesus to return.

Some people have claimed to have had near-death experiences, saying that they have gone to heaven, seen it, and visited loved ones. Now I want to be very careful not to offend anyone, but we must concern ourselves with what the Bible says, not the impressions or feelings of people.

The Bible has the best answer to this issue. It records at least nine resurrections from the dead, and in none of those cases is there a recorded story of the afterlife. Repeatedly, the Bible clearly says that when we die, we sleep awaiting the resurrection at Jesus' return. There is no consciousness and no recognition of time. It will be like one of those nights when you lay your head on the pillow and close your eyes and your alarm goes off moments later, but eight hours have passed. We will fall asleep, and the next moment all who have fallen asleep in Jesus will awake to that last trumpet.

So there is no need for us to be afraid of death or of what happens after we die. As we give our hearts and lives to Jesus, we are secure in Him and never have to fear. Jesus promises, "Do not be afraid; I am the First and the Last. I am He who lives, and was dead, and behold, I am alive forevermore. Amen. And I have the keys of Hades and of Death" (Revelation 1:17, 18). Jesus defeated death, and He is coming again to destroy death and sin forever. In the kingdom of heaven we will live with Him forever. Don't you want to fully trust yourself to His promises? Why not decide to follow Him completely today?

CHAPTER 5

So When Does It All Happen?

Annie Shapiro was fifty years old in 1963. While watching the coverage of John F. Kennedy's assassination on her black-and-white TV, she had a massive stroke and fell into a deep coma. Her husband, Martin Shapiro, dedicated to his wedding vows, spent the next thirty years bathing, changing, and dressing his wife. He would comb her hair and brush her teeth. He would give her eye drops every few hours to keep her eyes from drying out. He slept next to her at night. He prayed for a miracle recovery. He went to great lengths to find some type of medical solution.

During her coma, her body began to break down as she got older. She had cataract surgery, a hip replacement, and even a hysterectomy. Mrs. Shapiro was a successful businesswoman before this tragedy beset her. She had been planning to open new businesses in Hamilton, Ontario. Now she just lay there, a shell of her former self.

The world went on during her coma: the moon landing happened, the Vietnam War ended, and technology advanced.

On October 14, 1992, Annie Shapiro wakened from

her comatose state. Martin Shapiro shares the story that on that day, while he lay next to his wife, she suddenly sat up and said, "Turn on the television; I want to watch *I Love Lucy*." Her whole world had changed. She had aged thirty years, and her husband, now eighty-one, looked like an old man. Her son, who was eighteen at the time of her stroke, was now forty-eight and had two children. Phones were now cordless. The whole world around her had completely changed. Martin said that the day she awoke, "It was like a dead person came to life."

When asked by the media why he did not put his wife in a nursing home, he answered quite simply, "When I married, I pledged to be with Anne in sickness and in health, and I stuck to my vow."

I believe each one of us is going to experience an awakening that is even more amazing than the one Annie Shapiro went through. We are going to find ourselves suddenly thrust into a whole new world that none of us can even begin to imagine.

The Bible announces in 1 Thessalonians 4:16, 17 that "the Lord Himself will descend from heaven with a shout, with the voice of an archangel, and with the trumpet of God. And the dead in Christ will rise first. Then we who are alive and remain shall be caught up together with them in the clouds to meet the Lord in the air. And thus we shall always be with the Lord." The second coming of Christ will be the most spectacular event ever to occur on this planet.

The Bible tells us that this event will be seen by every

living person. "Behold, He is coming with clouds, and every eye will see Him, even they who pierced Him" (Revelation 1:7).

All of the death, all of the murders, all of the sin-filled darkness of this planet will end in a dramatic fashion, and we will enter a new state of being that we have never before experienced. The coming of Jesus Christ will be the climactic close to a chapter in this earth's history. Those who have died and are sleeping in Jesus will awaken from their graves, and it will be as if time stood still. Like Annie Shapiro, they will not know that a day or an hour has gone by. They will be alive again; but unlike Annie, they will not have broken-down bodies. Their new bodies will be completely healthy, optimal in operation.

Sadly, for some people, the awakening from the grave will not be good news. The arrival of God's kingdom will be truly tragic news for them. The Bible teaches that two awakenings from the grave will happen that lead to very different outcomes.

Jesus described it this way: "Do not marvel at this; for the hour is coming in which all who are in the graves will hear His voice and come forth—those who have done good, to the resurrection of life, and those who have done evil, to the resurrection of condemnation" (John 5:28, 29). Human beings that lived throughout history will be resurrected from their sleep of death at one of the two resurrections. Jesus' words are quite clear: "All who are in the graves will hear His voice."

The two resurrections are (1) the resurrection of life and

(2) the resurrection of condemnation. We do not want any part of the resurrection of condemnation. Revelation 20:6 states the promise that we want to be fulfilled for us: "Blessed and holy is he who has part in the first resurrection." This resurrection will be made up of the faithful people throughout the generations. In contrast, the remainder of the dead—those who were unfaithful—will be raised at a later time.

As we have continually asked whether heaven is for real, we also must ask, What will happen to those who are a part of the first resurrection?

Revelation 20:6 also promises that for those awakened in that first resurrection, "over such the second death has no power, but they shall be priests of God and of Christ, and shall reign with Him a thousand years."

The first resurrection, called the resurrection of life, will be the moment that the dead in Christ are transformed from corruptible to incorruptible, and they will be caught up to meet Jesus in the sky. Where will they go from there? They will travel with Jesus to heaven. But they will not be the only ones who will go on that journey. All the faithful followers of Jesus who are alive at His second coming will join in this parade to heaven.

This is the moment we are waiting for: "Behold, I tell you a mystery: We shall not all sleep, but we shall all be changed—in a moment, in the twinkling of an eye, at the last trumpet. For the trumpet will sound, and the dead will be raised incorruptible, and we shall be changed. For this corruptible must put on incorruption, and this mortal must put on immortality" (1 Corinthians 15:51–53). That day will fulfill Paul's prediction in 2 Timothy 4:8, "Finally, there is laid up for me the crown of righteousness, which the Lord, the righteous Judge, will give to me on that Day, and not to me only but also to all who have loved His appearing."

On that day, our mortal bodies that age and die will be made perfect, never to age and die again. We will rise toward Jesus and will travel to heaven with those raised from the dead. We will leave behind an earth that has been decimated by the upheaval of the natural world at the coming of Jesus. The wicked who will be dead will stay dead, and the wicked who will be alive—those who will have rejected the love of God and all of His attempts to woo them to Him—will die and remain on this planet. Revelation 6:15–17 tells of their demise: "The kings of the earth, the great men, the rich men, the commanders, the mighty men, every slave and every free man, hid themselves in the caves and in the rocks of the mountains, and said to the mountains and rocks, 'Fall on us and hide us from the face of Him who sits on the throne and from the wrath of the Lamb! For the great day of His wrath has come, and who is able to stand?'" They would stand to face Jesus if they loved Him, but instead they will have rejected His pleas to accept mercy and forgiveness. They will have rejected His outstretched arms and chosen not to be rescued by the Lamb of God who takes away the sins of the world.

The love of God is like the sun. If you take two bowls

and put butter in one and clay in the other, and then put them out in the sun, what happens? The butter melts, but the clay hardens. These are the two reactions that people have to the love of God. Paul puts it this way: "For the message of the cross is foolishness to those who are perishing, but to us who are being saved it is the power of God" (1 Corinthians 1:18). It is the same message, but it has two very different reactions.

For those who reject salvation, the message of Jesus and His death to save us is foolishness, is a myth, and does not awaken any change in their lives. But to others, the good news is the power of God that changes their lives forever. I want that good news to be the power of God in my life. Don't you?

So at the coming of Jesus, those who have experienced the power of God in their lives, who have had a transformational relationship with Jesus, will be taken up from this sin-stricken planet to go to heaven. Those who are alive and have seen the message of Jesus as foolishness and have rejected the message of the cross will be slain by the brightness of His coming.

What will happen to this earth on that day? Revelation 20:1, 2 tells us what will happen to the forces of evil. "Then I saw an angel coming down from heaven, having the key to the bottomless pit and a great chain in his hand. He laid hold of the dragon, that serpent of old, who is the Devil and Satan, and bound him for a thousand years." In Christianity, this thousand-year period is often referred to as the millennium. While the word *millennium* does not occur in the Bible, it is a Latin construction: *mille*, which means a thousand and *annum*, which means year. It is simply a descriptive word for this time period. What will happen during that thousand years? Satan and his angels will be bound in the bottomless pit.

What is this bottomless pit? In looking at the original Greek, we see that the phrase "bottomless pit" is the translation of the Greek word *Abussos*. From it, we get the English word *abyss*. It is also the same word used in Genesis 1:2 that describes the earth as being formless and empty.

The earth after Jesus' coming will be in a completely devastated state. It will have gone through so much turmoil that it will be in an almost "de-created" state. Satan will be "chained" to the earth through the chains of circumstance. He will not leave the devastated, empty planet.

The prophet Jeremiah describes the earth in this *Abussos* state:

> I beheld the earth, and indeed it was without form, and void;
> And the heavens, they had no light.
> I beheld the mountains, and indeed they trembled,
> And all the hills moved back and forth.
> I beheld, and indeed there was no man,
> And all the birds of the heavens had fled.
> I beheld, and indeed the fruitful land was a wilderness,
> And all its cities were broken down
> At the presence of the LORD,
> By His fierce anger.

Is Heaven for Real?

For thus says the LORD:

> "The whole land shall be desolate;
> Yet I will not make a full end" (Jeremiah 4:23–27).

Later the Lord tells Jeremiah, "And at that day the slain of the LORD shall be from one end of the earth even to the other end of the earth. They shall not be lamented, or gathered, or buried; they shall become refuse on the ground" (Jeremiah 25:33). Satan will be exiled to the devastated earth, "chained to the abyss," as the Bible says (see Revelation 20:2, 3), and no one will be alive except the devil and his angels. There will be no people to tempt into sin and no one to hurt and harm. He will have a thousand years to contemplate his life of complete rebellion.

In the utter destruction of this planet, one timeless principle will be echoed again and again: the wages of sin is death. And looking on, the whole universe will bear witness to the terrible truth of those words. The devil will be confronted with the horrible results of his rebellion.

Let us focus on the more positive aspects of the thousand years. What joyous things will the righteous be doing with Jesus? Remember that Revelation 20:6 said that we will be priests of God, reigning with Him for a thousand years. It is almost unimaginable how amazing that will be. Even so, we will have some questions. I once heard it said that we will be surprised by three things in heaven: (1) that we are there, (2) who is not there, and (3) who is there. You may ask, "Why is Uncle So-and-So not here?"

or "Where is Pastor So-and-So? He seemed like such a good person." Or maybe you will wonder how a particular person could possibly be there because he or she was so unkind to you.

Jesus will answer every one of those questions. During the thousand years, we will inspect all of God's decisions in the judgment. The almighty Creator of the universe will allow you and me to review His work! John tells us, "I saw thrones, and they sat on them, and judgment was committed to them" (Revelation 20:4). And Paul says, "Do you not know that the saints will judge the world? And if the world will be judged by you, are you unworthy to judge the smallest matters? Do you not know that we shall judge angels? How much more, things that pertain to this life?" (1 Corinthians 6:2, 3). We will look over the cases of the saved and the lost. Something to keep in mind is that we will not judge anything or anyone until that time. Paul instructs us, "Therefore judge nothing before the time, until the Lord comes, who will both bring to light the hidden things of darkness and reveal the counsels of the hearts. Then each one's praise will come from God" (1 Corinthians 4:5). Every hidden and secret thing will eventually be brought to light. We cannot hide anything from God.

It will be revealed in those days why God could not save some people. We will see the choices that individuals made to reject the love of God. We will see every way He tried to reach out, to what great extent He pursued every individual in history with His gifts for them. At the end of it all, we will only have one conclusion. "Even so, Lord

God Almighty, true and righteous are Your judgments" (Revelation 16:7).

Moreover, each of us will be able to understand fully why we experienced what we did in life. We will see the entire road map that God took us on, and we will see that His plan was perfect.

At the end of the thousand years, the Bible says that Satan will be released from his prison, and the second resurrection will happen. We will look at those events in the next chapter. For the saved ones in heaven, they will experience even more joy at the end of the thousand years. God will restore earth to its perfect Edenic beauty, back to what He created in the beginning. John describes this marvelous event: "Now I saw a new heaven and a new earth, for the first heaven and the first earth had passed away. Also there was no more sea. Then I, John, saw the holy city, New Jerusalem, coming down out of heaven from God, prepared as a bride adorned for her husband" (Revelation 21:1, 2).

This is a description of our return trip from heaven. We will be in the city of the New Jerusalem—in that mansion Jesus said He is preparing for us—and He will bring us back to the earth that He will make new again. The city will fly down to earth with us in it! "And I heard a loud voice from heaven saying, 'Behold, the tabernacle of God is with men, and He will dwell with them, and they shall be His people. God Himself will be with them and be their God'" (verse 3).

God will reclaim this planet as His own and restore

it to its perfect beauty. He is making our home now, and our home will be with Him. In the vast universe, God will choose to make His dwelling here, on the once-rebellious planet. What a privilege for us, and what a joy to be able to live with God forever!

When we wake up at the Second Coming, God will give us new bodies and restored minds that will last forever. No more disabilities and limitations, no missing limbs, and no blindness, just perfect health and perfect harmony. Jesus wants to save you so that His power can change you. The experience of heaven will be something you'll never want to miss. It comes down to one very simple decision. Will you yield your life to the One who gave His life on Mount Calvary? Is heaven for real? It is real. And it will be the grandest time that anyone can ever experience. It comes down to a decision to believe and have faith in Jesus who died for you and me. Will you believe? Will you place your trust in Jesus?

CHAPTER 6

What About Hell?

Salmon Arm, British Columbia, is a beautiful city in the southern interior portion of the province. Nestled on the shores of Shuswap Lake, with a stunning view of Bastion Mountain, it is a popular tourist destination. The beaches and recreational activities make it a memorable vacation spot.

In 1998, however, you would not have wanted to be in Salmon Arm. That year saw one of the warmest, driest, and longest summers ever recorded in Canada. The droughtlike conditions led to one of the worst fire seasons on record. The Fly Hills near Salmon Arm were ignited by natural causes, and the fire quickly became unmanageable and moved toward Salmon Arm. The dense forest with plenty of fuel to burn provided a path for the flames to head toward the city. Despite efforts by the Ministry of Forests and local firefighters, the flames could not be controlled. Many watched their homes and their lifework go up in smoke. Others watched and wondered when the disaster would finally stop. By the time it was over, approximately ten million dollars had been spent to extinguish the blaze. More than 6,000 hectares (14,826 acres) were burned, 40 buildings were destroyed, and more than 7,000 people had been evacuated.

It is almost impossible to imagine the heat and destructive power of those flames, but the vivid pictures of the burning landscape seem to conjure up an apocalyptic scene. The book of Revelation paints a similar picture of apocalyptic flames: "He [the devil] shall be tormented with fire and brimstone in the presence of the holy angels and in the presence of the Lamb. And the smoke of their torment ascends forever and ever; and they have no rest day or night, who worship the beast and his image, and whoever receives the mark of his name" (Revelation 14:10, 11). A little later in this book, John reveals more when speaking of the destruction of spiritual Babylon. "Again they said, 'Alleluia! Her smoke rises up forever and ever!'" (Revelation 19:3).

The burning forests of Salmon Arm give us a preview of the final enormous fire that will destroy the earth. And in asking whether heaven is for real, we now must turn and ask, Is hell for real? Just as thousands prayed and hoped that the flames of Salmon Arm (and countless other wildfires) would stop, what about the fires of hell? What does it mean that the smoke ascends "forever and ever"? Will the final destruction of the wicked be an endless, ongoing inferno of pain?

So far in this book we have found the Bible's evidence that heaven is a very real place. Jesus has prepared a place for us, and He has made every provision for us to be there. But what about those who choose not to go to heaven?

Is Heaven for Real?

Because of their actions, thoughts, and deeds, will they burn in torment forever and ever? We already know that the dead are not experiencing any pain right now but are sleeping in the grave. What will happen when Jesus comes again?

When Jesus returns, the righteous who are ready for Him will be made incorruptible—perfect. Those who died while following Jesus will be resurrected and given new bodies, and those still alive will be changed in an instant. Then we will be with Jesus in heaven for the millennium. But on the day that Jesus comes, the wicked who died before will stay dead, with the exception of one small, select group. John says, "Behold, He is coming with clouds, and every eye will see Him, *even they who pierced Him*" (Revelation 1:7; emphasis added). That select group is made up of the people directly responsible for the death of Christ around A.D. 33. They will be resurrected to see Jesus come back. But they will be alive for only a short time. As Jesus approaches this earth, all of the wicked who are still alive will be slain by the brightness of His coming. All of the dead will remain on the earth for a thousand years.

At the end of the thousand years, when the New Jerusalem descends from heaven to the earth, the wicked will be all raised. The Bible explains what will happen next:

Now when the thousand years have expired, Satan will be released from his prison and will go out to deceive the nations which are in the four corners of the earth, Gog and Magog, to gather them together to battle, whose number is as the sand of the sea. They went up on the breadth of the earth and surrounded the camp of the saints and the beloved city. *And fire came down from God out of heaven and devoured them.* The devil, who deceived them, was cast into the lake of fire and brimstone where the beast and the false prophet are. And they will be tormented day and night forever and ever (Revelation 20:7–10; emphasis added).

This clear picture of hell is not of a place somewhere in faraway space. The lake of fire is on this earth. And Satan and the wicked are destroyed in it. In the Bible, this destruction is called the second death.

Now I must pause for a moment. We find in this passage an amazing picture of God. Many have portrayed Him as a great tormentor who is out to get us. The picture of God that has sometimes been painted by the church is that He is waiting for you to make one mistake so He can zap you. This picture is not painted by the Bible but by writings such as Dante's *Inferno*, stories in Greek mythology, and ancient Egyptian religion. This is not the picture that the Bible portrays at all.

We may ask, "Why is there hellfire at all?" Matthew 25:41 makes it absolutely clear why hellfire exists: "Then He will also say to those on the left hand, 'Depart from Me, you cursed, into the everlasting fire prepared for the devil and his angels.'" Hellfire was "prepared for the devil and his angels." *It was never intended for any human being.* It was created to take care of the author of sin—Satan. Now God could not and would not destroy Satan immediately when he rebelled. By doing so, God would have risked having a universe of created beings who served Him out of fear rather than love. But the Lord allowed Satan to run his full course so that beings everywhere could see the sinfulness of sin and the horrible nature of the devil's rebellion. So why are humans included in hellfire? Because the lake of fire is intended to put an end to all traces of sin once and for all. Humans will end up in the lake of fire because they have so attached themselves to their sin and are so unwilling to let it go that they must be burned up with their sin.

This may be a new idea to you, but that means hellfire is a one-time event that destroys sin, suffering, pain, the devil and his angels, along with the wicked who cling to their sin—never to exist again. Death is gone forever. The consequence is permanent.

The Bible does not describe an ever-burning place of torment where we will be able to see or hear the agony of the wicked; in fact, quite the opposite. Revelation 21 describes the new heaven and new earth.

> Now I saw a new heaven and a new earth, for the first heaven and the first earth had passed away. Also there was no more sea. Then I, John, saw the holy city, New Jerusalem, coming down out of heaven from God, prepared as a bride adorned for her husband. And I heard a loud voice from heaven saying,

What About Hell?

"Behold, the tabernacle of God is with men, and He will dwell with them, and they shall be His people. God Himself will be with them and be their God. And God will wipe away every tear from their eyes; there shall be no more death, nor sorrow, nor crying. There shall be no more pain, for the former things have passed away" (verses 1–4).

This is the complete picture of the re-created earth. There is no sectioned-off corner for an ever-burning hell—only the wonderful promise of a new heaven and a new earth. There will be no death, no dying, no pain, no sorrow, and no separation. Everything will be made new. How could you combine that with an ever-burning hell where people agonize in pain? The reality is that you cannot.

The fire of Salmon Arm consumed anything in its path. If you look at before-and-after pictures of the forest fire, it is truly astonishing. Nothing is left—nothing. The fire of Salmon Arm serves as a lesson on the lake of fire of Revelation. There will be nothing left.

What happens to those who are thrown into a lake of fire? How long will they survive? Typically, the bigger the fire, the quicker the burn. If you want to torture someone for a long time, you need a very small flame, not a great lake of fire. Could the Bible be trying to tell us something by calling this lake of fire the second death?

We have to allow the Bible to speak for itself on the subject of hell. Listen to what it says in Malachi 4:1,

"For behold, the day is coming,
Burning like an oven,
And all the proud, yes, all who do wickedly will be
stubble.
And the day which is coming shall burn them up,"
Says the LORD of hosts,
"That will leave them neither root nor branch."

Malachi did not speak of people being continually roasted on a hellfire spit. They will be burned up like stubble, which disappears into nothing.

So Scripture is very clear that, first of all, hell is in the future, and, second, the wicked will be burned up to nothing on that day. Hell is not happening now in some central hot spot of the earth or out in the universe. After the thousand years, the wicked will be consumed and turned to ashes—burned up completely.

This is the consistent teaching of Scripture on the subject:

- "You shall make them as a fiery oven in the time of Your anger; the LORD shall swallow them up in His wrath, and the fire shall devour them" (Psalm 21:9).
- "Behold, they shall be as stubble, the fire shall burn them; they shall not deliver themselves from the power of the flame" (Isaiah 47:14).
- "The wicked shall perish; and the enemies of the LORD, like the splendor of the meadows, shall

vanish. Into smoke they shall vanish away" (Psalm 37:20).

• "You shall trample the wicked, for they shall be ashes under the soles of your feet" (Malachi 4:3).

Why does Revelation speak of the smoke of their torment going up "forever and ever"? Other verses may help us understand the subject more clearly. Here is one example: "Not with the blood of goats and calves, but with His own blood He entered the Most Holy Place once for all, having obtained eternal redemption" (Hebrews 9:12). Now Jesus died once for our sins. His great act of redemption took place at a specific time and place. In addition, the final judgment happens at a specific time. Neither of these goes on forever and ever, although the results are permanent and everlasting. It is the same with hellfire. It has permanent and everlasting consequences.

The short book of Jude is even more explicit in explaining this: "As Sodom and Gomorrah, and the cities around them in a similar manner to these, having given themselves over to sexual immorality and gone after strange flesh, are set forth as an example, suffering the vengeance of eternal fire" (verse 7). Sodom and Gomorrah are famous for having been completely wiped off the face of the earth by fire from heaven. No trace of the cities or the people remained. They are an example of what the destiny of the wicked will be. Have you seen on the news or in a video on the internet that some city near the Dead Sea is continually burning, never to be extinguished? No, but the Bible tells us, "And turning the cities of Sodom and Gomorrah into ashes, condemned them to destruction, making them an example to those who afterward would live ungodly" (2 Peter 2:6).

The Bible is consistent in its portrayal of hellfire and rejects Greek myths and other sources of the eternally raging inferno. It is consistently clear that hellfire is eternal from the standpoint that its consequences are permanent and everlasting. Everything thrown into the lake of fire will be turned to ashes. Here is the end of the wicked, according to Paul: "For many walk, of whom I have told you often, and now tell you even weeping, that they are the enemies of the cross of Christ: whose end is destruction" (Philippians 3:18, 19). Literally, the meaning of the Greek word for "destruction" is annihilation.

Romans 6:23 says that "the wages of sin is death." This death is the second death: permanent separation from God because you no longer exist. Jesus Himself said, "Do not fear those who kill the body but cannot kill the soul. But rather fear Him who is able to destroy both soul and body in hell" (Matthew 10:28). Destruction is what the lake of fire brings—total and utter destruction.

Some scriptures that seem to allude to a place of everlasting punishment are simply metaphors to describe the permanent nature of hellfire. Jesus on one occasion used such an illustration.

> If your hand causes you to sin, cut it off. It is better for you to enter into life maimed, rather than having

two hands, to go to hell, into the fire that shall never be quenched—where

> *"Their worm does not die*
> *And the fire is not quenched"* (Mark 9:43, 44; emphasis added).

Many people today point to this as evidence of an eternally burning hell. But is that really what this means?

Jesus is quoting a passage in Isaiah 66, where the prophet quotes God's description of the fate of the wicked and uses those phrases, "Their worm does not die, and their fire is not quenched" (verse 24). But what is God referring to? Here is the first part of verse 24, which precedes those phrases: "And they shall go forth and look upon the corpses of the men who have transgressed against Me." While it is a bit morbid, this passage is a picture of worms consuming dead bodies. The corpses are being totally consumed, totally destroyed. What about "their fire is not quenched"? An unquenchable fire is one that cannot be put out. Again this describes the permanent results of the fire. If the fire could be quenched, there would be a possibility of someone living after it is gone. But this fire cannot be quenched; it destroys completely. The people are burned up. So even in these phrases we are talking about corpses being destroyed once and forever.

The prophet Jeremiah uses a similar device in describing the destruction of Jerusalem. God said, "Then I will kindle a fire in its gates, and it shall devour the palaces of

Jerusalem, and it shall not be quenched" (Jeremiah 17:27). Is Jerusalem still on fire today? No, because at the time this prophecy was fulfilled, Jerusalem was burned to the ground. Its destruction was permanent, and the fire that destroyed it could not be put out.

In the midst of these stark truths, it is a good idea to remind ourselves of God's motive. "Beloved, do not forget this one thing, that with the Lord one day is as a thousand years, and a thousand years as one day. The Lord is not slack concerning His promise, as some count slackness, but is longsuffering toward us, not willing that any should perish but that all should come to repentance" (2 Peter 3:8, 9). Our loving God is doing everything He possibly can to save each one of us. You do not need to worry about hellfire, because it was not designed for you. It is the destiny of the devil and his angels. The open arms of Jesus are the destiny He has for you.

Are you willing to let go of your sin and give yourself to Jesus? He wants to save you, and right now He is working on your behalf to make sure that happens. Accept His invitation of love today. He is calling for you, and He is knocking at your heart's door. Will you open it and let Him in?

CHAPTER 7

How Long Is Forever?

Let us go on a journey to the southeastern corner of the Dead Sea in modern-day Jordan. Archaeologists have uncovered a site along the southeastern banks of the Dead Sea, which they believe to be the location of Sodom and Gomorrah, though there is not 100 percent assurance. They found a site with more than 1.5 million graves, which indicates a thriving population. The famed archaeologist Nelson Glueck worked in the area and discovered a trade route from ancient Mesopotamia to Sodom and Gomorrah. The trade with other cities accounts at least in part for their wealth and luxury. At this site, we find the approximate location of the ancient cities of Sodom and Gomorrah. At one time, they were amazing cities, wealthy and luxurious, but filled with gross immorality. Scholars and archaeologists believe that ancient Sodom and Gomorrah were part of a metropolis that consisted of five cities, each having its own king. This was a population center that reflected great wealth and sophistication. In addition, outside of the cities lay very fertile ground that provided excellent crops for food. Studies have revealed that they grew an abundance of grains and plentiful orchards.

Wine flowed freely, and wickedness increased. The people of these cities turned their backs on God. They were only concerned with indulging in immoral pleasures. But they soon would encounter the judgment of God.

The population had become corrupt, and they were warned of their impending doom. The people refused to change. The Bible tells us, "The LORD rained brimstone and fire on Sodom and Gomorrah, from the LORD out of the heavens" (Genesis 19:24).

As archaeologists excavated the site, they found signs of absolute destruction and a thick layer of ash. This evidence of a city destroyed by fire in Abraham's time is a phenomenal corroboration of God's holy Word.

Genesis 18:20 describes the cities' sin as being "grave," but in one of these cities lived a servant of God—Lot and his family. Lot was the nephew of Abraham.

God invited Lot to escape with his life. Two angels visited him and led his family out of those wicked cities. On their way out, Lot's wife looked back. Her heart was still in the city, still attached to the pleasures and the wealth. She could not leave her old self behind and enjoy the new life that God had planned.

Today, Jesus makes the same invitation to you and me, that we lay down anything that separates us from Him and escape, leaving all our earthly, materialistic attachments behind to live lives devoted to Him. Lot's wife looked back and died. She was lost eternally. God calls us today to be genuine Christians and have life-transforming relationships with Him. We cannot straddle the fence. We need to be all in for Jesus.

Fire fell on those cities, and it is worth reading again the lesson of Sodom and Gomorrah: "As Sodom and Gomorrah, and the cities around them in a similar manner to these, having given themselves over to sexual immorality and gone after strange flesh, are set forth as an example, suffering the vengeance of eternal fire" (Jude 7).

Sodom and Gomorrah were absolutely destroyed. They do not continue to burn, but rather they were turned to ash, like burned stubble. This serves as an example of what hell will be at the end of the thousand years. These cities were full of immorality; they partied; and they practiced sexual relationships outside the confines of marriage. They received plenty of warning, but God finally said that their time was up. A day is coming soon when the cup of rebellion and sin will be full here on this earth, and God will say, "That is enough." He wants to save as many as possible, and He is going to intervene in this earth's history to assure that there will be a faithful remnant—a faithful final group that He will take home to heaven. For those who do not want to be part of the heavenly realm, God in His mercy removes them from existence by destruction with fire after the millennium.

The Bible describes eternal fire as a permanent result. Sodom and Gomorrah never burned again. The destruction was complete, and the effects were eternal. That is the consistent picture we get from the teachings of Jesus and the Bible writers. Death, utter destruction, is the ultimate fate of the wicked.

Some believe and teach that Satan and sinners will be tormented "forever and ever." The basis for such a belief is not in the Bible. It is rooted in ancient Egyptian religion, which was passed on to the Greeks, and it entered the church through Roman paganism.

Some will point to a text such as Revelation 20:10, "The devil, who deceived them, was cast into the lake of fire and brimstone where the beast and the false prophet are. And they will be tormented day and night forever and ever." The phrase "forever and ever" in the Greek can literally mean "until the end of the age." Think about what an ever-burning hell would require. If you have ever been burned, you know it is very painful. But being thrown into a fire would lead to death. An ever-burning fire would require God to keep an individual alive and only partly burned, over and over again, so they could continue to suffer. This does not fit in with the character of God. The wicked will be consumed completely. Satan and his angels will be utterly destroyed, and the results will be eternal.

"Forever" in the Bible often denotes a limited time—for example, as long as one lives. Exodus 21:6 says, "Then his [a servant's] master shall bring him to the judges. He shall also bring him to the door, or to the doorpost, and his master shall pierce his ear with an awl; and he shall serve him forever." The servant could not serve after he or his master died, so this use of "forever" means for a lifetime. As long as the slave lived, he would serve.

How Long Is Forever?

Jonah used "forever" when he described being swallowed by the fish:

"I went down to the moorings of the mountains;
The earth with its bars closed behind me forever;
Yet You have brought up my life from the pit,
O LORD, my God" (Jonah 2:6).

Although it may have seemed like forever to him at the time, Jonah was in the belly of the fish for the allotted time of three days. Likewise, in 1 Samuel 1:22, Hannah dedicated Samuel to serve the Lord in the temple and remain there "forever." Verse 28 clarifies the meaning: "Therefore I also have lent him to the LORD; as long as he lives he shall be lent to the LORD." As long as he lives—this is "forever."

The vivid and graphic images of eternal fire and smoke rising forever emphasize the tragedy of losing those who turn from God. The Bible says of this time of destruction, that God will "bring to pass His act, His unusual act" (Isaiah 28:21). This is God's "unusual act." The English Standard Version of the Bible states it, "To do his deed—strange is his deed! And to work his work—alien is his work!" The King James Version says, "That he may do his work, his strange work; and bring to pass his act, his strange act." So the destruction of the wicked is called unusual, strange, and alien. God is a creator, not a destroyer. He will only have to remove sin once.

God wants to create a new heart in you. You do not need

to worry about hell because you have the opportunity to serve Him and follow Him and be with Him. Serve Him out of love and not fear. Even those who choose not to follow Him will not be punished for an eternity over one lifetime of mistakes and bad choices. God in His mercy will simply destroy these people in an instant.

Even so, we will not want to have any part in that event after the millennium. Jesus said, "Cast them into the furnace of fire. There will be wailing and gnashing of teeth" (Matthew 13:50). And in Matthew 22, Jesus describes going to heaven as a great wedding banquet. There is a wonderful celebration. But someone comes unprepared, not wearing the wedding garment, which is a reference to not being covered in the righteousness of Christ. Because of this guest's great presumption, he is cast away. "Then the king said to the servants, 'Bind him hand and foot, take him away, and cast him into outer darkness; there will be weeping and gnashing of teeth'" (Matthew 22:13). Those who rejected Him will suddenly realize the import of what they chose, and they will wail in great agony at the thought.

A similar picture appears in Matthew 25:30. In the parable of the ten talents, the lazy servant who did not put his talent to work for the master receives this sentence: "Cast the unprofitable servant into the outer darkness. There will be weeping and gnashing of teeth." Why such pain? Because in each case, those who rejected Jesus realize what they have missed—they are cut off from the wonderful reward. Missing out on eternal life will be the greatest tragedy in history. That is the agony of hell.

How Long Is Forever?

The master describes his reward to the faithful servant in Matthew 25:21, "His lord said to him, 'Well done, good and faithful servant; you were faithful over a few things, I will make you ruler over many things. Enter into the joy of your lord.'" The joy of our Lord is to be in heaven with each of us for eternity.

Does God need to arbitrarily torture the wicked in order to punish them adequately? Absolutely not! The real pain comes to them through the realization of what they have missed, what they have thrown away. There is nothing in this life that can compare with the bliss and peace of heaven. They realize that they have thrown it all away for a few moments of pleasure, and it was not worth it at all. No wonder there is weeping and gnashing of teeth.

We have concluded from the Bible that hell is not a place but an event on this earth that brings an end to sin forever. This is the merciful act of a loving God who must bring all things to a close.

One Bible passage that has raised questions about the topic is 1 Peter 3:19, which says, "He went and preached to the spirits in prison." The easiest way to understand this text is to read the surrounding verses.

For Christ also suffered once for sins, the just for the unjust, that He might bring us to God, being put to death in the flesh but made alive by the Spirit, by whom also He went and preached to the spirits in prison, who formerly were disobedient, when once the Divine longsuffering waited in the days of Noah, while the ark was being prepared, in which a few, that is, eight souls, were saved through water. There is also an antitype which now saves us—baptism (not the removal of the filth of the flesh, but the answer of a good conscience toward God), through the resurrection of Jesus Christ, who has gone into heaven and is at the right hand of God, angels and authorities and powers having been made subject to Him (verses 18–22).

First, verse 18 shows that Jesus was made alive by the Spirit, so Jesus is not dead in this passage. Who then are these "spirits in prison," and when did Jesus preach to them? Verse 20 makes it clear that Peter means the people from the days of Noah. Christ spoke at that time through the prophets to the people, most of whom were possessed by evil spirits of violence and immorality. He tried to release them from their bondage of sin and provided every opportunity for them to repent and break their bonds. There was no visiting an eternal burning center of the earth. Jesus, through the prophets, spoke to the people in Noah's day and tried to release them from their "prison" of sin.

Now others will say, "Wait; what about the story of the rich man and Lazarus?" It is found in Luke 16:19–31.

There was a certain rich man who was clothed in purple and fine linen and fared sumptuously every day. But there was a certain beggar named Lazarus, full of sores, who was laid at his gate, desiring to be fed with the crumbs which fell from the rich man's table. Moreover the dogs came and licked his sores. So it was that the beggar died, and was carried by the angels to Abraham's bosom. The rich man also died and was buried. And being in torments in Hades, he lifted up his eyes and saw Abraham afar off, and Lazarus in his bosom.

Then he cried and said, "Father Abraham, have mercy on me, and send Lazarus that he may dip the tip of his finger in water and cool my tongue; for I am tormented in this flame." But Abraham said, "Son, remember that in your lifetime you received your good things, and likewise Lazarus evil things; but now he is comforted and you are tormented. And besides all this, between us and you there is a great gulf fixed, so that those who want to pass from here to you cannot, nor can those from there pass to us."

Then he said, "I beg you therefore, father, that you would send him to my father's house, for I have five brothers, that he may testify to them, lest they also come to this place of torment." Abraham said to him, "They have Moses and the prophets; let them hear them." And he said, "No, father Abraham; but if one goes to them from the dead, they will repent." But he said to him, "If they do not hear Moses and the prophets, neither will they be persuaded though one rise from the dead."

Is Heaven for Real?

The first important point is that this is a parable in a string of parables through which Jesus taught about the kingdom of God. Often parables are symbolic or metaphorical in nature and are used to illustrate a point. It is not possible to take each point of the parable literally. If we were to do so, then we would literally go to Abraham's bosom to reach heaven (how big would his bosom have to be?). This is, of course, only an illustration. What a terrible place heaven would be if we had continual contact with those who were lost. In this parable, Jesus used a story common among the Jews that described dying as passing through a dark valley and finding salvation in fleeing to the bosom of Abraham. The people of that time also thought that the rich were the blessed ones of God and were surely going to heaven. So Jesus used this parable to turn things on end.

He then used the parable to teach three distinct points: First, any wealth gained by greed or through dishonesty or by disregarding the poor is not a sign of having God's favor. Second, there is no second chance after death. Once you have lived your life and you die, it is over. Third, Jesus had given sign upon sign, including raising someone from the dead, and yet many of the religious leaders rejected Him. Had they studied their Scriptures, the Old Testament, with an open mind, they would have known that Jesus was the promised Messiah. Their refusal to study the Word kept them from accepting Jesus, even with all the signs in the world.

We do not need to be like the Pharisees or Sadducees.

How Long Is Forever?

We can accept Jesus and the miracle of His love. On the cross, Jesus suffered the full consequences of the second death. He did that so we would not have to and we could live forever with Him. Heaven is for real, and He wants to take us there.

All we must do is place our faith in Christ as Savior and entrust our lives into His hands. Won't you make your choice today?

CHAPTER 8

Is Heaven for Real? Choose Life

Is heaven for real? The testimony of the Bible is that heaven is a very real place that is assured to those who choose to spend their lives with Jesus.

John 14:1–4 shows us the heart cry of Jesus: "Let not your heart be troubled; you believe in God, believe also in Me. In My Father's house are many mansions; if it were not so, I would have told you. I go to prepare a place for you. And if I go and prepare a place for you, I will come again and receive you to Myself; that where I am, there you may be also. And where I go you know, and the way you know."

Scripture continues,

Thomas said to Him, "Lord, we do not know where You are going, and how can we know the way?"

Jesus said to him, "I am the way, the truth, and the life. No one comes to the Father except through Me.

"If you had known Me, you would have known My Father also; and from now on you know Him and have seen Him" (verses 5–7).

Jesus is the Way; He is the only way to heaven. And Jesus desires to give us life abundant. In John 10:10, Jesus says, "I have come that they may have life, and that they may have it more abundantly." Jesus' desire for each one of us is to have a life of abundant living in Him that leads to eternal life.

He has made the provision for each of us to be rid of the guilt and shame of our sin. He is the One who has made a way for us to be reconciled to Him. The last book of the Bible, the book of Revelation, is really the revelation of Jesus Christ. It tells the story of Jesus and His faithfulness to save us from our sin and make the path clear to heaven. Heaven is for real; and Jesus has done, is doing, and will do everything He can to assure your place there.

It is in this vein that the Messiah is introduced in Revelation 1:5, 6 as

Jesus Christ, the faithful witness, the firstborn from the dead, and the ruler over the kings of the earth.

To Him who loved us and washed us from our sins in His own blood, and has made us kings and priests to His God and Father, to Him be glory and dominion forever and ever.

In addition, verse 8 says, " 'I am the Alpha and the Omega, the Beginning and the End,' says the Lord, 'who is and who was and who is to come, the Almighty.' "

Jesus has always been and always will be the One who wants to save us. He walks among the churches; He walks among the people. He knows you, and He knows me. He knows our trials and knows the burdens of our lives. He understands us and makes a way for us.

Jesus is pictured throughout Revelation with various symbols and metaphors—the only One who can open a scroll for our redemption, the Babe of Bethlehem, and the conquering King. Revelation 14:14 says, "Then I looked, and behold, a white cloud, and on the cloud sat One like the Son of Man, having on His head a golden crown, and in His hand a sharp sickle." He is pictured again in Revelation 19:11, "Now I saw heaven opened, and behold, a white horse. And He who sat on him was called Faithful and True, and in righteousness He judges and makes war." In Revelation 21 and 22, He is the One who makes all things new for our home in heaven with Him. Jesus boldly states in Revelation 22:7, 12, and 20 the threefold promise that He is coming quickly. He is coming soon to take us home.

The key in all of this and the key for our success in this life is found in Revelation 12:11, "And they overcame him [Satan] by the blood of the Lamb and by the word of their testimony, and they did not love their lives to the death." Over and over again in Scripture and especially in Revelation, Jesus is pictured as a Lamb.

When you think of mighty animals, you do not typically think of a lamb. But the Lamb is the Victor in the book of Revelation. Revelation 17:14 makes it very clear: "These will make war with the Lamb, and the Lamb will overcome them, for He is Lord of lords and King of kings; and those who are with Him are called, chosen, and faithful."

Is Heaven for Real? Choose Life

The Lamb is a symbol of Christ, the innocent One who died on the cross for you and for me to make a way for us to be reconciled to God. The Lamb wins. This is the profound message of the Bible, reaching its pinnacle in the book of Revelation. As long as we are for the Lamb, Jesus, we will be victorious with Him.

I would like for us to take a journey back in time. The story and names are only for illustrative purposes. Let us go back in time to the tent of Ariel. Ariel is up early in the morning, and he begins walking through the encampment of Israel. Tents are here and there. He walks leading a lamb. This lamb is perfect and spotless. He and his family have raised this lamb since it was born.

Ariel is taking this lamb as a sacrifice. That it is a sacrifice for sin is at the forefront of his mind. There is only one way to reconcile with God, and it is to take the life of this little lamb.

Ariel arrives at the entrance to the sanctuary, where he is greeted by a priest. He takes that little lamb into the courtyard and places his hands on the head and confesses his sin. After he symbolically transfers his sin to that lamb, the throat of the lamb is slit. It is swift and merciful, but the blood of the animal is spilled. The priest takes the lamb and places it on the altar of burnt offering.

Ariel sees the smoke arising to heaven. This little lamb pointed forward to the true sacrifice that would be given by the perfect Messiah. Ariel has been forgiven, not because of the loss of that animal's life but because of his trust in God that this sacrifice pointed forward to Jesus.

The sanctuary service helped people to take personal responsibility for their own sin. It also pointed out that forgiveness came from outside of themselves and could only be administered by God. They needed His divine grace to experience forgiveness. The sacrificing of the lamb was an act of faith that Jesus was the One who takes away all the sins of the world.

John the Baptist testified to Jesus being that Lamb: "John saw Jesus coming toward him, and said, 'Behold! The Lamb of God who takes away the sin of the world!'" (John 1:29). Jesus was the fulfillment of the symbol of the spotless lamb.

Scripture is very clear in Romans 6:23, "The wages of sin is death." And in Romans 3:23 it says, "All have sinned and fall short of the glory of God." We are in desperate need of a Savior. Without Jesus we have one destiny—death. And not just death in a grave but eternal death, which is permanent separation from God.

The Old Testament sacrifice pointed forward to Jesus. The guilt of a sinner was symbolically removed in the sacrificial service. Now all we need to do is to confess our sins, and they are placed upon Jesus and we are forgiven. First John 1:9 promises, "If we confess our sins, He is faithful and just to forgive us our sins and to cleanse us from all unrighteousness." Forgiven and cleansed, we are freed in the arms of Jesus. He was born and died as the penalty for our sin.

Jesus Christ died on the cross as a sacrifice for our sin. That is the only sacrifice that cleanses us and makes us whole. Jesus is the only way. There are not multiple routes. Christ paid the price as the perfect Lamb of God. He was victorious over sin. He lived a perfect life and, as an innocent sacrifice, paid the price for us. And His victory brings divine forgiveness in our lives.

We need forgiveness today. Guilt will rob a person of peace and happiness and security. The death of Jesus removes that guilt when we confess our sins to Him. We often try all kinds of different ways to relieve our guilt and shame. But the only forgiveness that truly can bring peace comes from one source, and that is Jesus Christ.

Our friends may try to bring comfort, but they cannot solve our guilt. Psychology can help us to adjust and cope, but it cannot deal with our guilt.

It took the Cross to create pardon and grace. Christ poured out His life on the cross, and He took on our guilt and gave us His righteousness, His right standing with the Father. That is why the sacrifice of the Lamb is so powerful—the Source of our great peace.

Paul makes this wonderful promise about Jesus in 2 Corinthians 5:21, "For He made Him who knew no sin to be sin for us, that we might become the righteousness of God in Him." Christ never sinned. He was perfect and lived a perfect life. But He made a choice. He never sinned but became sin for us. He assumed the guilt of us all and all our sin, but He never committed one sin.

We find peace in Jesus. We do not deserve it, and we have not earned it, but Jesus offers it freely. We find the peace of Jesus Christ by reaching out in faith and asking

Jesus to forgive us and be our Savior.

Our sin required the death of Jesus so we might live. It is our sin that required this great sacrifice—and our lives that Jesus wants to rescue. He wants to take us to heaven to live with Him forever. His death has made that path clear.

The story of the Bible is that Jesus, the Lamb of God, wins. He cannot be defeated. We have been given a view of the end. We know how the story ends. He has given us everything. We are guaranteed a victory. Listen to these words of 1 Peter 1:18, 19: "Knowing that you were not redeemed with corruptible things, like silver or gold, from your aimless conduct received by tradition from your fathers, but with the precious blood of Christ, as of a lamb without blemish and without spot." We are not saved by our wealth, by our possessions, or by our good deeds. We cannot earn salvation through working harder. We are saved by Jesus alone, by the blood of the Lamb. It is through Him that we can live victorious lives.

Salvation is a gift from Jesus. He offers it to us, and all we have to do is accept it by faith. For many of us, this is hard to understand, not because it is complicated but because of how our lives have been shaped. Many of us have tried to earn the approval or acceptance of others. We have spent our whole lives seeking that acceptance from a mother or father, or maybe from a spouse or some love interest. We have done this or done that to earn love, but Jesus says No, salvation is a gift from God. The grace of Jesus Christ is a gift; His forgiveness is a gift. We may nod our heads in agreement that it is a gift, but we try to earn it. Today Jesus is calling to our hearts to accept this simple, life-giving gift, to stop the rat race of trying to earn His love and accept that which He has freely given. He desires this real experience for us that we might be prepared for the reality of heaven. So how can we receive and have the assurance of this free gift of salvation?

The first step is to accept and know that God loves you and longs to save you. Jeremiah 31:3 gives this wonderful promise: "The Lord has appeared of old to me, saying: 'Yes, I have loved you with an everlasting love; therefore with lovingkindness I have drawn you.'" God has everlasting love for you and for me. This is the reality. We first must come to terms with and accept that reality. No matter what you have done, who your family is, whether you are rich or poor—He loves you with an everlasting love.

And then we need to realize that we cannot earn our salvation or save ourselves. Romans 3:23, 24 makes this clear: "For all have sinned and fall short of the glory of God, being justified freely by His grace through the redemption that is in Christ Jesus." We are sinners and cannot save ourselves; there is nothing we can do. We are justified or simply saved by Jesus Christ. He alone is the way to salvation. In accepting that, we need to really believe that Jesus can and will save us. Romans 10:9 says, "If you confess with your mouth the Lord Jesus and believe in your heart that God has raised Him from the dead, you will be saved." It is a guarantee, a promise that will not fail.

Then we confess our sin to Jesus. "If we confess our sins,

Is Heaven for Real?

He is faithful and just to forgive us our sins and to cleanse us from all unrighteousness" (1 John 1:9). There are no conditions other than confessing. We tell Jesus who we are and what we have done, and then He forgives us. We no longer have to pay the price for our own sin; we accept His sacrifice on our behalf. But not only that, He cleanses us—He helps us to have lives that are clean and pure.

And last, we live and claim this gift; 1 John 5:11, 12 assures us, "This is the testimony: that God has given us eternal life, and this life is in His Son. He who has the Son has life; he who does not have the Son of God does not have life." We have life with Jesus.

Is heaven for real? It is absolutely real, and Jesus is coming to take us home to this place of everlasting peace. Jesus says that He is the way to heaven. He has made every provision necessary for you to be there. The good news of the gospel has always been available to us. It is a free gift to those who come. Jesus came and lived here, He died and rose again, and He defeated the grave so you and I can have eternal life. In one of the last appeals of the Bible, we receive this strong invitation: "The Spirit and the bride say, 'Come!' And let him who hears say, 'Come!' And let him who thirsts come. Whoever desires, let him take the water of life freely" (Revelation 22:17).

Heaven is for real, and it will be the home of those who accept the salvation of Jesus Christ freely. Will you accept that gift today?

Jesus is life. He is our peace in a time of trouble. When we choose Jesus, He is our strength, even in our weakness.

Is Heaven for Real? Choose Life

When our world is crumbling around us and the whole world seems shaken to the core, Jesus renews us and gives us life. He alone can give that life. He is light in our dark world. Jesus is the One. His amazing sacrifice of love gives us life. That life is a renewed life now and eternal life in the future. What He has done for you, what He has done for me, is truly amazing.

It's easy to learn more about the Bible!

Call:
1-888-456-7933

Write:
Discover
P.O. Box 999
Loveland, CO 80539

FREE Lessons at www.BibleStudies.com

In Canada
Call:
905-404-6510

Write:
It Is Written Canada
P.O. Box 2010
Oshawa, ON L1H 7V4

www.itiswrittencanada.ca/bible-studies